Simple Air Fryer Cookbook for One

⟵──────────────⟶

Easy Healthy and Flavor Recipes With Stunning Photos

By Kayla D. Rojas

Copyright © 2024 By Kayla D. Rojas

All rights reserved.No part of this publication may be reproduced, distributed, or transmitted in any form or by any means, including photocopying, recording, or other electronic or mechanical methods, without the prior written permission of the publisher, except in the case of brief quotations embodied in critical reviews and specific other noncommercial uses permitted by copyright law. For permission requests, write to the publisher, addressed "Attention: Permissions Coordinator," at the address below.

Kayla D. Rojas asserts the moral right to be identified as the author of this work.

This book is a work of non-fiction based on the author's experiences and research on the subject. All efforts have been made to ensure accuracy and compliance with Kindle Direct Publishing (KDP) rules and regulations. However, the publisher and author do not assume and, at this moment, disclaim any liability to any party for any loss, damage, or disruption caused by errors or omissions, whether such errors or omissions result from negligence, accident, or any other cause.

This publication is designed to provide accurate and authoritative information regarding the subject matter covered. It is sold with the understanding that the publisher and author are not engaged in rendering professional services. If expert assistance is required, the services of a competent professional should be sought.

Introduction

Introduction for "Simple Air Fryer Cookbook for One: Easy Healthy and Flavor Recipes With Stunning Photos" by Kayla D. Rojas

Welcome to "Simple Air Fryer Cookbook for One," where your journey into delightful, easy, and healthy cooking begins. This book, crafted by Kayla D. Rojas, is more than just a cookbook; it's a gateway to a new lifestyle that embraces the simplicity and efficiency of using an air fryer for solo dining.

Imagine having a personal culinary guide that understands the nuances of cooking for one. Each recipe in this book has been meticulously tested and tailored to fit your needs, ensuring you can enjoy a variety of flavors without the hassle of adjusting portions or dealing with leftovers. From quick breakfasts to delectable dinners, these recipes are designed to fit seamlessly into your busy life.

Picture yourself effortlessly preparing meals that nourish your body and please your palate. The air fryer's magic lies in its ability to cook meals quicker and healthier without sacrificing taste. Whether you are a seasoned cook or just beginning your culinary journey, this book is filled with recipes that will inspire you to explore new flavors and techniques. Accompanied by stunning photos, each dish becomes an achievable masterpiece, turning everyday cooking into an extraordinary experience.

Dive into "Simple Air Fryer Cookbook for One" and start enjoying the art of cooking for yourself. This book, available in Kindle and Paperback formats, adheres to Kindle Direct Publishing's rules and regulations, ensuring a high-quality, easy-to-follow culinary adventure. Grab your copy today and embark on a journey of culinary discovery, where each meal is a celebration of simplicity, health, and flavor.

Table of Contents

Chapter-01: Chicken Recipes 6
- Recipe-01: Fried Chicken Wings With Lemon Garlic Chilli Herbs & Spices 6
- Recipe-02: Sticky Honey-Soy Chicken Wings 8
- Recipe-03: Teriyaki Glazed Chicken Wings 10
- Recipe-04: Buffalo Chicken Tenders With Celery And Blue Cheese 12
- Recipe-05: Roast Chicken With Brussel Sprouts 14
- Recipe-06: Italian Chicken Parmesan With Cheese And Sauce 16
- Recipe-07: Chicken Souvlaki With Parsley And Lime Wedges 18
- Recipe-08: Cajun Spice Roasted Chicken 20
- Recipe-09: Thai Ginger Chicken 22
- Recipe-10: Fresh Buttermilk Soaked Fried Chicken Thighs 24

Chapter-02: Fish Recipes 26
- Recipe-11: Breaded Fish Fillet 26
- Recipe-12: Roasted Salmon With Herbs 28
- Recipe-13: Cajun Tilapia With Cauliflower And Pasta 30
- Recipe-14: Crab & Pumpkin Crusted Mahi Mahi With Asparagus And Calamansi Butter 32
- Recipe-15: Grilled Sea Bass 34
- Recipe-16: Grilled Fresh Spicy Prawns Shrimps With Lime And Oregano 36
- Recipe-17: Halibut With Hazelnut Crust With Roast Red Pepper Sauce 38
- Recipe-18: Red Curry With Salmon In Coconut Milk Sauce 40
- Recipe-19: Trout With Crispy Almond Crust And Baked Mashed Potatoes 42
- Recipe-20: Roasted Swordfish With Leek Ginger And Sesame Seed 44

Chapter-03: Meat Recipes 46
- Recipe-21: Juicy Sliced Beef Ribeye Steak 46
- Recipe-22: Roasted Beef Steak Striploin Juicy Mustard Sauce 48
- Recipe-23: Grilled Lamb Mutton Meat Chops Steaks 50
- Recipe-24: Bacon Wrapped Sirloin Steak With Herbs 52
- Recipe-25: Korean Bulgogi Beef 54
- Recipe-26: Boneless Pork Chops BBQ 56
- Recipe-27: Garlic Butter Steak Bites 58
- Recipe-28: Freshly Honey Maple Glazed Ham 60

Recipe-29: Chipotle Grilled Flank Steak 62

Recipe-30: Honey Mustard Chicken Thighs With Herbs 64

Chapter-04: Seafood Recipes 66

Recipe-31: Crispy Calamari Rings With Lemon Wedge 66

Recipe-32: Stir-Fried Lobster With Butter & Garlic Sauce 68

Recipe-33: Fried Coconut Shrimp On A Skewer With A Dipping Sauce 70

Recipe-34: Fish Beer Batter And Chips With Green Pea And Tartar Sauce 72

Recipe-35: Homemade Maryland Crab Cakes 74

Recipe-36: Scalloped Lemon Garlic Butter Sauce Grilled 76

Recipe-37: Bang Bang Shrimps 78

Recipe-38: Grilled Octopus With Pesto And Lime 80

Recipe-39: Stuffed Mushrooms With Salmon And Cream 82

Recipe-40: Grilled Oysters With Lemon Garlic 84

Chapter-05: Snacks Recipes 86

Recipe-41: Crispy Deep Fried Potato Wedges With Herbs 86

Recipe-42: Fried Mozzarella Sticks With Marinara Sauce 88

Recipe-43: Buffalo Cauliflower Bites With Sauce 90

Recipe-44: Pizza Rolls Puff Pastry Stuffed With Prosciutto Bacon 92

Recipe-45: Loaded Taters Tots With Cheese And Bacon 94

Recipe-46: Breaded Fried Avocado Fries With Chipotle Sauce 96

Recipe-47: Deep Fried Tornado Potato 98

Recipe-48: Fried Cheese Breaded Zucchini With Sour Cream 100

Recipe-49: Pies Filo Pastry With Chicken And Spinach 102

Recipe-50: Fried Chicken Spring Rolls 104

Chapter-01: Chicken Recipes

Recipe-01: Fried Chicken Wings With Lemon Garlic Chilli Herbs & Spices

Medium   **Cooking: 20 Mins**   **Servings: 01**   **Prep: 15 Mins**

INTRODUCTION

Introducing a mouth-watering recipe for "Fried Chicken Wings with Lemon Garlic Chilli Herbs and Spices," perfect for all Air Fryer enthusiasts. This dish combines the zest of lemon, the heat of chili, and a blend of herbs and spices, resulting in a flavor-packed meal that's sure to delight.

INGREDIENTS

- ✓ 6 chicken wings
- ✓ 1 tsp of lemon zest
- ✓ 2 cloves of garlic, minced
- ✓ 1 tsp of chili flakes
- ✓ 1 tsp of mixed herbs (thyme, oregano, rosemary)
- ✓ Salt and pepper to taste
- ✓ 1 tbsp olive oil

COOKING STEPS

1. Combine lemon zest, minced garlic, chili flakes, mixed herbs, salt, pepper, and olive oil in a bowl.
2. Toss the chicken wings in the marinade, ensuring they are well coated.
3. Preheat the Air Fryer to 180°C (356°F).
4. Place the wings in the Air Fryer basket, ensuring they're not overcrowded.
5. Cook for 20 minutes, turning halfway through, until golden and crispy.

NUTRITIONAL FACTS: (PER SERVING)

- ❖ Calories: 310 kcal
- ❖ Protein: 24g
- ❖ Fat: 22g
- ❖ Carbohydrates: 2g

FINAL WORD

To conclude, these Fried Chicken Wings with Lemon Garlic Chilli Herbs and Spices are not just another chicken recipe; they celebrate flavors and textures. Air frying ensures a healthier option without compromising the crispy, golden exterior. Whether you're cooking for one or a group, this dish will impress!

Recipe-02: Sticky Honey-Soy Chicken Wings

Medium | **Cooking: 25 Mins** | **Servings: 01** | **Prep: 10 Mins**

INTRODUCTION

Embark on a culinary journey with "Sticky Honey-Soy Chicken Wings," a delectable Air Fryer chicken recipe that's both sweet and savory. This dish is perfect for those who love a combination of honey's sweetness and the umami richness of soy sauce, all wrapped around succulent chicken wings.

INGREDIENTS

- ✓ 6 chicken wings
- ✓ 2 tbsp honey
- ✓ 1 tbsp soy sauce
- ✓ 1 garlic clove, minced
- ✓ 1/2 tsp ginger, grated
- ✓ 1 tsp sesame seeds
- ✓ Salt and pepper, to taste

COOKING STEPS

1. Mix honey, soy sauce, minced garlic, grated ginger, sesame seeds, salt, and pepper in a bowl.
2. Add chicken wings to the mixture, coating them evenly.
3. Preheat the Air Fryer to 190°C (374°F).
4. Place the wings in the Air Fryer basket, ensuring they don't overlap.
5. Air fry for 25 minutes, flipping halfway through, until they are sticky and golden.

NUTRITIONAL FACTS: (PER SERVING)

- ❖ Calories: 330 kcal
- ❖ Protein: 23g
- ❖ Fat: 18g
- ❖ Carbohydrates: 18g

FINAL WORD

In summary, these Sticky Honey-Soy Chicken Wings are a perfect blend of sweet and savory, making them an irresistible treat. The Air Fryer method offers a healthier alternative to traditional frying, ensuring a delicious meal without the extra oil. Ideal for a quick dinner or a special weekend treat, these wings are sure to be a hit!

Recipe-03: Teriyaki Glazed Chicken Wings

Easy | **Cooking: 25 Mins** | **Servings: 01** | **Prep: 15 Mins**

INTRODUCTION

Savor the rich and savory flavors of "Teriyaki Glazed Chicken Wings," a must-try Air Fryer recipe. These wings are glazed in a homemade teriyaki sauce, offering a perfect balance of sweet and tangy flavors. Ideal for those who appreciate the depth of Japanese cuisine, this dish is easy to prepare and delightful to the palate.

INGREDIENTS

- ✓ 6 chicken wings
- ✓ 2 tbsp teriyaki sauce
- ✓ 1 tbsp honey
- ✓ 1 tsp garlic, minced
- ✓ 1/2 tsp ginger, grated
- ✓ Sesame seeds for garnish
- ✓ Salt to taste

COOKING STEPS

1. Mix teriyaki sauce, honey, minced garlic, grated ginger, and salt in a bowl.
2. Marinate the chicken wings in the mixture for at least 30 minutes.
3. Preheat the Air Fryer to 200°C (392°F).
4. Place the wings in the Air Fryer basket, spacing them evenly.
5. Cook for 25 minutes, turning halfway, until they are beautifully glazed and cooked through.

NUTRITIONAL FACTS: (PER SERVING)

- ❖ Calories: 340 kcal
- ❖ Protein: 25g
- ❖ Fat: 20g
- ❖ Carbohydrates: 15g

FINAL WORD

To wrap up, these Teriyaki Glazed Chicken Wings are a simple yet delicious way to taste Japan from your kitchen. The Air Fryer ensures a healthier version of this popular dish, retaining all the flavors while reducing the oil. Perfect for a solo meal or as a part of a shared feast, these wings are guaranteed to impress!

Recipe-04: Buffalo Chicken Tenders With Celery And Blue Cheese

Medium | **Cooking: 20 Mins** | **Servings: 01** | **Prep: 10 Mins**

INTRODUCTION

Dive into the bold flavors of "Buffalo Chicken Tenders with Celery and Blue Cheese," a classic dish reimagined for the Air Fryer. This recipe offers the perfect blend of spicy Buffalo sauce and cooling blue cheese paired with crisp celery. It's an ideal choice for those craving a tangy meal, delivering all the taste with the convenience of air frying.

INGREDIENTS

- ✓ 4 chicken tenders
- ✓ 1/4 cup Buffalo sauce
- ✓ 1 tbsp olive oil
- ✓ 2 celery stalks, sliced
- ✓ 2 tbsp blue cheese, crumbled
- ✓ Salt and pepper, to taste

COOKING STEPS

1. Preheat the Air Fryer to 200°C (392°F).
2. Season chicken tenders with salt and pepper.
3. Lightly brush the tenders with olive oil and place them in the Air Fryer basket.
4. Cook for 10 minutes, flip, and cook for another 10 minutes until golden and crisp.
5. Toss the cooked tenders in Buffalo sauce.
6. Serve with sliced celery and crumbled blue cheese on top.

NUTRITIONAL FACTS: (PER SERVING)

- ❖ Calories: 380 kcal
- ❖ Protein: 28g
- ❖ Fat: 22g
- ❖ Carbohydrates: 8g

FINAL WORD

Wrapping up, these Buffalo Chicken Tenders with Celery and Blue Cheese combine the best spicy and creamy flavors in one dish. The Air Fryer offers a healthier alternative to deep frying, keeping the chicken juicy and crispy outside. This dish is perfect for a satisfying meal or a crowd-pleasing appetizer, guaranteed to tantalize your taste buds.

Recipe-05: Roast Chicken With Brussel Sprouts

Moderate | **Cooking: 35 Mins** | **Servings: 01** | **Prep: 15 Mins**

INTRODUCTION

Experience the home-cooked goodness of "Roast Chicken with Brussels Sprouts, Carrot, and Potato," a delightful recipe that brings the traditional roast dinner into the realm of Air Fryer cooking. This dish offers a wholesome blend of tender chicken and roasted vegetables, creating a comforting and nutritious meal perfect for any day of the week.

INGREDIENTS

- ✓ 1 chicken breast
- ✓ 1/2 cup Brussels sprouts, halved
- ✓ 1 carrot, sliced
- ✓ 1 small potato, cubed
- ✓ 1 tbsp olive oil
- ✓ 1 tsp mixed herbs (rosemary, thyme, parsley)
- ✓ Salt and pepper, to taste

COOKING STEPS

1. Preheat the Air Fryer to 180°C (356°F).
2. Season the chicken breast with salt, pepper, and mixed herbs.
3. Toss Brussels sprouts, carrot, and potato with olive oil, salt, and pepper in a bowl.
4. Place the chicken and vegetables in the Air Fryer basket.
5. Cook for 35 minutes until the chicken is cooked and the vegetables are tender.

NUTRITIONAL FACTS: (PER SERVING)

- ❖ Calories: 420 kcal
- ❖ Fat: 15g
- ❖ Protein: 30g
- ❖ Carbohydrates: 40g

FINAL WORD

In conclusion, this Roast Chicken with Brussels Sprouts, Carrot, and Potato recipe is a fantastic way to enjoy a classic roast healthier and more conveniently. The Air Fryer ensures that each component is perfectly cooked, offering a satisfying blend of flavors and textures. Whether you're cooking for one or looking for a simple family dinner, this dish will indeed become a favorite.

Recipe-06: Italian Chicken Parmesan With Cheese And Sauce

Medium | **Cooking: 25 Mins** | **Servings: 01** | **Prep: 20 Mins**

INTRODUCTION

Indulge in the classic flavors of Italy with "Italian Chicken Parmesan with Cheese and Sauce," a delicious Air Fryer recipe that brings a beloved Italian-American dish to your table. This recipe features a succulent chicken breast coated in crispy breadcrumbs and smothered with tangy tomato sauce and melted cheese, creating a delectable fusion of flavors to satisfy your cravings.

INGREDIENTS

- ✓ 1 chicken breast, flattened
- ✓ 1/4 cup breadcrumbs
- ✓ 1/4 cup grated Parmesan cheese
- ✓ 1/2 cup marinara sauce
- ✓ 1/4 cup shredded mozzarella cheese
- ✓ 1 egg, beaten
- ✓ Salt and pepper, to taste
- ✓ 1 tsp Italian seasoning

COOKING STEPS

1. Preheat the Air Fryer to 190°C (374°F).
2. Season the chicken with salt, pepper, and Italian seasoning.
3. Dip the chicken in the beaten egg, then coat with breadcrumbs and Parmesan cheese.
4. Place the chicken in the Air Fryer and cook for 15 minutes.
5. Top the chicken with marinara sauce and mozzarella cheese.
6. Cook for another 10 minutes until the cheese is melted and bubbly.

NUTRITIONAL FACTS: (PER SERVING)

- ❖ Calories: 500 kcal
- ❖ Fat: 20g
- ❖ Protein: 40g
- ❖ Carbohydrates: 35g

FINAL WORD

This Italian Chicken Parmesan with Cheese and Sauce recipe is a delightful way to enjoy a restaurant-quality meal at home. The Air Fryer method offers a healthier approach to this classic dish, ensuring a crispy exterior and tender interior. Perfect for a cozy dinner for one or a special occasion, this dish promises a truly satisfying Italian culinary experience.

Recipe-07: Chicken Souvlaki With Parsley And Lime Wedges

Easy | **Cooking: 15 Mins** | **Servings: 01** | **Prep: 30 Mins**

INTRODUCTION

Embark on a culinary journey to the Mediterranean with "Chicken Souvlaki with Parsley and Lime Wedges," a delightful Air Fryer recipe. This dish features succulent chicken pieces marinated in aromatic herbs and spices and then perfectly cooked. Served with fresh parsley and zesty lime wedges, it's a light yet flavorful meal that brings a taste of Greece to your kitchen.

INGREDIENTS

- ✓ 200g chicken breast, cut into cubes
- ✓ 2 tbsp olive oil
- ✓ 1 tbsp lemon juice
- ✓ 1 garlic clove, minced
- ✓ 1/2 tsp dried oregano
- ✓ Salt and pepper, to taste
- ✓ Fresh parsley, chopped for garnish
- ✓ Lime wedges for serving

COOKING STEPS

1. Mix olive oil, lemon juice, minced garlic, oregano, salt, and pepper in a bowl.
2. Marinate the chicken cubes in the mixture for at least 1 hour.
3. Preheat the Air Fryer to 200°C (392°F).
4. Thread the marinated chicken onto skewers.
5. Cook in the Air Fryer for 15 minutes, turning halfway, until golden and cooked through.
6. Garnish with chopped parsley and serve with lime wedges.

NUTRITIONAL FACTS: (PER SERVING)

- ❖ Calories: 310 kcal
- ❖ Protein: 26g
- ❖ Fat: 20g
- ❖ Carbohydrates: 3g

FINAL WORD

In conclusion, this Chicken Souvlaki with Parsley and Lime Wedges recipe is a simple yet exquisite way to enjoy a Greek classic. The Air Fryer provides a healthier alternative to traditional grilling, ensuring juicy and tender chicken with a delightful char. This dish will become a regular in your cooking repertoire, perfect for a quick, nutritious meal.

Recipe-08: Cajun Spice Roasted Chicken

Easy | **Cooking: 30 Mins** | **Servings: 01** | **Prep: 10 Mins**

INTRODUCTION

Delight in the bold and zesty flavors of "Cajun Spice Roasted Chicken," an irresistible Air Fryer recipe. This dish celebrates Cajun cuisine, featuring a blend of spices that bring a lively kick to the tender, juicy chicken. Perfect for spice lovers and those looking to add some excitement to their meal routine, this recipe is both easy to prepare and irresistibly delicious.

INGREDIENTS

- ✓ 1 chicken breast
- ✓ 1 tsp paprika
- ✓ 1/2 tsp garlic powder
- ✓ 1/2 tsp onion powder
- ✓ 1/4 tsp cayenne pepper
- ✓ 1/4 tsp dried thyme
- ✓ 1/4 tsp dried oregano
- ✓ Salt and pepper, to taste
- ✓ 1 tbsp olive oil

COOKING STEPS

1. Mix paprika, garlic powder, onion powder, cayenne pepper, thyme, oregano, salt, and pepper in a small bowl.
2. Rub the chicken breast with olive oil, then coat evenly with the spice mix.
3. Preheat the Air Fryer to 180°C (356°F).
4. Place the chicken in the Air Fryer basket and cook for 30 minutes or until the internal temperature reaches 75°C (165°F).

NUTRITIONAL FACTS: (PER SERVING)

- ❖ Calories: 220 kcal
- ❖ Fat: 11g
- ❖ Protein: 26g
- ❖ Carbohydrates: 2g

FINAL WORD

Concluding, this Cajun Spice Roasted Chicken offers a delightful way to enjoy the rich flavors of Southern cooking with the convenience of an Air Fryer. The perfect blend of spices ensures each bite is flavorful, making this dish a standout choice for a quick and satisfying meal. Whether you're a fan of Cajun cuisine or just looking to try something new, this recipe will surely impress.

Recipe-09: Thai Ginger Chicken

Medium   **Cooking: 20 Mins**   **Servings: 01**   **Prep: 15 Mins**

INTRODUCTION

Embark on a culinary adventure with "Thai Ginger Chicken," a vibrant and flavorful Air Fryer recipe that blends Thai cuisine's aromatic essence with modern cooking's convenience. This dish is a harmonious mix of tender chicken, zesty ginger, and exotic spices. It creates a stimulating and satisfying meal for those who love exploring international flavors in their kitchen.

INGREDIENTS

- ✓ 1 chicken breast, cut into strips
- ✓ 1 tbsp fresh ginger, grated
- ✓ 2 cloves garlic, minced
- ✓ 1 tbsp soy sauce
- ✓ 1 tbsp oyster sauce
- ✓ 1 tsp honey
- ✓ 1 tsp sesame oil
- ✓ Fresh cilantro for garnish
- ✓ Lime wedges for serving

COOKING STEPS

1. Mix ginger, garlic, soy sauce, oyster sauce, honey, and sesame oil in a bowl.
2. Marinate the chicken strips in the mixture for at least 30 minutes.
3. Preheat the Air Fryer to 190°C (374°F).
4. Place the chicken in the Air Fryer basket and cook for 20 minutes, turning halfway, until golden and cooked through.
5. Garnish with fresh cilantro and serve with lime wedges.

NUTRITIONAL FACTS: (PER SERVING)

- ❖ Calories: 275 kcal
- ❖ Fat: 9g
- ❖ Protein: 28g
- ❖ Carbohydrates: 15g

FINAL WORD

In summary, this Thai Ginger Chicken recipe is a fantastic way to enjoy the exotic flavors of Thai cuisine in a simple, healthy manner. The Air Fryer ensures quick and easy cooking, making this dish ideal for a flavorful weekday dinner or a special occasion. It's a delightful meal that will transport your taste buds to the streets of Bangkok!

Recipe-10: Fresh Buttermilk Soaked Fried Chicken Thighs

Medium   **Cooking: 25 Mins**   **Servings: 01**   **Prep: 150 Mins**

INTRODUCTION

Indulge in the ultimate comfort food with "Fresh Buttermilk Soaked Fried Chicken Thighs," a delectable Air Fryer recipe. This dish features chicken thighs soaked in buttermilk for tenderness and coated in a perfectly seasoned crust. The result is a delightful contrast of crispy exterior and juicy interior, bringing a beloved classic into your kitchen with a healthier twist.

INGREDIENTS

- ✓ 2 chicken thighs
- ✓ 1 cup buttermilk
- ✓ 1 cup all-purpose flour
- ✓ 1 tsp paprika
- ✓ 1 tsp garlic powder
- ✓ 1/2 tsp black pepper
- ✓ Salt to taste
- ✓ Cooking spray

COOKING STEPS

1. Marinate chicken thighs in buttermilk for at least 3 hours.
2. Preheat the Air Fryer to 180°C (356°F).
3. Mix flour, paprika, garlic powder, black pepper, and salt in a bowl.
4. Remove chicken from the buttermilk and dredge in the flour mixture.
5. Spray the Air Fryer basket with cooking spray and place the chicken thighs.
6. Cook for 25 minutes, turning halfway, until golden and crispy.

NUTRITIONAL FACTS: (PER SERVING)

- ❖ Calories: 490 kcal
- ❖ Fat: 22g
- ❖ Protein: 35g
- ❖ Carbohydrates: 35g

FINAL WORD

These Fresh buttermilk-soaked fried Chicken Thighs offer a mouth-watering fusion of crispy, golden texture and moist, flavorful meat. The Air Fryer method provides a healthier alternative to traditional frying, allowing you to enjoy this classic comfort food without the guilt. Perfect for a cozy night in or a special weekend treat, this recipe is sure to satisfy your cravings.

Chapter-02: Fish Recipes

Recipe-11: Breaded Fish Fillet

Medium | **Cooking: 15 Mins** | **Servings: 01** | **Prep: 10 Mins**

INTRODUCTION

Discover the delicious simplicity of "Breaded Fish Fillet," a classic Air Fryer fish recipe that's both effortless and satisfying. This dish features a delicate fish fillet coated in a crispy, golden breadcrumb layer, creating a perfect blend of textures and flavors. Ideal for those seeking a quick, healthy seafood option, this recipe will become a staple in your culinary repertoire.

INGREDIENTS

- ✓ 1 fish fillet (such as cod or tilapia)
- ✓ 1/2 cup breadcrumbs
- ✓ 1 egg, beaten
- ✓ 1/2 tsp paprika
- ✓ Salt and pepper, to taste
- ✓ Lemon wedges for serving

COOKING STEPS

1. Season the fish fillet with salt, pepper, and paprika.
2. Dip the fillet in the beaten egg, then coat with breadcrumbs.
3. Preheat the Air Fryer to 200°C (392°F).
4. Place the breaded fillet in the Air Fryer basket.
5. Cook for 15 minutes or until the breadcrumb coating is crispy and golden.

NUTRITIONAL FACTS: (PER SERVING)

- ❖ Calories: 285 kcal
- ❖ Fat: 9g
- ❖ Protein: 23g
- ❖ Carbohydrates: 25g

FINAL WORD

In conclusion, this Breaded Fish Fillet recipe is a delightful way to enjoy fish in a healthy yet indulgent manner. The Air Fryer ensures a crispy texture without excessive oil, making it an excellent quick and nutritious meal option. Served with a squeeze of fresh lemon, it's a dish that promises both simplicity and flavor.

Recipe-12: Roasted Salmon With Herbs

Easy | **Cooking: 10 Mins** | **Servings: 01** | **Prep: 05 Mins**

INTRODUCTION

Embrace the sublime flavors of the sea with "Roasted Salmon with Herbs," a splendid Air Fryer fish recipe. This dish features a succulent salmon fillet seasoned with a medley of herbs that enhance its natural richness. Ideal for a sophisticated yet easy-to-prepare meal, it's perfect for health-conscious gourmets and seafood lovers alike, offering a balance of simplicity and gourmet flair.

INGREDIENTS

- ✓ 1 salmon fillet (about 150g)
- ✓ 1/2 tsp dried dill
- ✓ 1/2 tsp dried parsley
- ✓ 1/4 tsp garlic powder
- ✓ Salt and pepper, to taste
- ✓ Lemon slices, for garnish

COOKING STEPS

1. Season the salmon fillet with dill, parsley, garlic powder, salt, and pepper.
2. Preheat the Air Fryer to 200°C (392°F).
3. Place the salmon in the Air Fryer basket, skin-side down.
4. Cook for 10 minutes until the salmon is cooked through and flakes easily with a fork.
5. Garnish with lemon slices before serving.

NUTRITIONAL FACTS: (PER SERVING)

- ❖ Calories: 280 kcal
- ❖ Protein: 23g
- ❖ Fat: 20g
- ❖ Carbohydrates: 0g

FINAL WORD

To conclude, this Roasted Salmon with Herbs recipe is a testament to the beauty of simplicity in cooking. The Air Fryer method ensures a moist, flaky texture while imbuing the salmon with the aromatic flavors of the herbs. Whether a quick weeknight dinner or a special occasion, this dish will impress with its elegant simplicity and exquisite taste.

Recipe-13: Cajun Tilapia With Cauliflower And Pasta

Medium

Cooking:20 Mins

Servings: 01

Prep: 15 Mins

INTRODUCTION

Dive into the vibrant world of Cajun cuisine with "Cajun Tilapia with Cauliflower and Pasta," an enticing Air Fryer fish recipe. This dish combines the spicy kick of Cajun seasoning, the delicate flavor of tilapia, and the hearty comfort of pasta and cauliflower. It's perfect for those who enjoy a bit of spice in their meals and are looking for a wholesome, flavorful dinner option.

INGREDIENTS

- ✓ 1 tilapia fillet
- ✓ 1/2 cup cauliflower florets
- ✓ 1 cup cooked pasta (your choice)
- ✓ 1 tsp Cajun seasoning
- ✓ 1 tbsp olive oil
- ✓ Salt and pepper, to taste
- ✓ Lemon wedges for serving

COOKING STEPS

1. Season the tilapia fillet with Cajun seasoning, salt, and pepper.
2. Toss the cauliflower florets with olive oil, salt, and pepper.
3. Preheat the Air Fryer to 180°C (356°F).
4. Place the tilapia and cauliflower in the Air Fryer basket.
5. Cook for 15 minutes or until the fish is cooked through and the cauliflower is tender.
6. Serve the cooked tilapia and cauliflower over the cooked pasta.
7. Garnish with lemon wedges.

NUTRITIONAL FACTS: (PER SERVING)

- ❖ Calories: 400 kcal
- ❖ Protein: 28g
- ❖ Fat: 15g
- ❖ Carbohydrates: 40g

FINAL WORD

This Cajun Tilapia with Cauliflower and Pasta recipe is a delightful blend of flavors and textures. The Air Fryer makes cooking quick and easy, ensuring a healthy yet satisfying meal. Whether you're a fan of Cajun cuisine or just exploring new flavors, this dish will surely provide a delicious and enjoyable dining experience.

Recipe-14: Crab & Pumpkin Crusted Mahi Mahi With Asparagus And Calamansi Butter

Advanced | **Cooking: 15 Mins** | **Servings: 01** | **Prep: 20 Mins**

INTRODUCTION

Experience a symphony of flavors with "Crab and Pumpkin Crusted Mahi Mahi with Asparagus and Calamansi Butter," an exquisite Air Fryer fish recipe. This dish offers a unique fusion of tastes, featuring the mild, sweet flavor of Mahi Mahi, enhanced by a rich crab and pumpkin crust and complemented by the fresh zest of asparagus and the tangy twist of Calamansi butter.

INGREDIENTS

- ✓ 1 Mahi Mahi fillet
- ✓ 1/4 cup crab meat
- ✓ 2 tbsp pumpkin puree
- ✓ 1/4 cup breadcrumbs
- ✓ 6 asparagus spears
- ✓ 2 tbsp butter
- ✓ 1 tsp Calamansi juice (or lime juice)
- ✓ Salt and pepper, to taste

COOKING STEPS

1. Preheat the Air Fryer to 200°C (392°F).
2. Mix crab meat, pumpkin puree, breadcrumbs, salt, and pepper. Spread this mixture over the Mahi Mahi fillet.
3. Place the crusted fillet and asparagus spears in the Air Fryer basket.
4. Cook for 15 minutes or until the fish is cooked and the crust is golden.
5. Melt butter and mix with Calamansi juice for the sauce.
6. Serve the fish and asparagus with the Calamansi butter drizzled on top.

NUTRITIONAL FACTS: (PER SERVING)

- ❖ Calories: 350 kcal
- ❖ Protein: 30g
- ❖ Fat: 18g
- ❖ Carbohydrates: 15g

FINAL WORD

This crab and pumpkin cured Mahi Mahi with asparagus, and Calamansi Butter is a gourmet delight that combines unique flavors and textures. The Air Fryer ensures a healthier preparation, preserving the fish's delicacy and the crust's crispness. This dish is a testament to culinary creativity, perfect for a special occasion or a luxurious weeknight treat.

Recipe-15: Grilled Sea Bass

Easy | **Cooking: 12 Mins** | **Servings: 01** | **Prep: 05 Mins**

INTRODUCTION

Embark on a delightful seafood journey with "Grilled Sea Bass," a simple yet elegant Air Fryer fish recipe. This dish highlights the delicate flavor of sea bass, enhanced by a light seasoning and the perfect grilling technique. Ideal for those who appreciate the natural taste of fresh fish with a hint of smokiness, it's a minimalistic approach to a gourmet dining experience.

INGREDIENTS

- ✓ 1 sea bass fillet
- ✓ 1 tbsp olive oil
- ✓ 1/2 tsp garlic powder
- ✓ 1/2 tsp paprika
- ✓ Salt and pepper, to taste
- ✓ Lemon slices, for garnish

COOKING STEPS

1. Preheat the Air Fryer to 200°C (392°F).
2. Rub the sea bass fillet with olive oil, garlic powder, paprika, salt, and pepper.
3. Place the fillet in the Air Fryer basket.
4. Cook for 12 minutes or until the fish is flaky and cooked through.
5. Garnish with lemon slices before serving.

NUTRITIONAL FACTS: (PER SERVING)

- ❖ Calories: 250 kcal
- ❖ Protein: 22g
- ❖ Fat: 16g
- ❖ Carbohydrates: 1g

FINAL WORD

In conclusion, this Grilled Sea Bass recipe is a testament to the beauty of simplicity in cooking. The Air Fryer technique provides a healthier alternative to traditional grilling, ensuring a perfectly cooked, juicy fillet with a hint of crispiness. Whether a quick weekday meal or a special dinner, this dish will impress with its straightforward elegance and delicious flavors.

Recipe-16: Grilled Fresh Spicy Prawns Shrimps With Lime And Oregano

Easy **Cooking:08 Mins** **Servings: 01** **Prep:15 Mins**

INTRODUCTION

Dive into the zesty and compelling world of "Grilled Fresh Spicy Prawns with Lime and Oregano," a vibrant Air Fryer fish recipe. This dish combines the juiciness of prawns with the fiery kick of spices, balanced by the refreshing notes of lime and oregano. It's perfect for those who love a bit of heat in their seafood, offering a flavor-packed experience that's both quick and delightful.

INGREDIENTS

- ✓ 6 large prawns (shrimps), deveined
- ✓ 1 tbsp olive oil
- ✓ 1/2 tsp chili flakes
- ✓ 1 tsp dried oregano
- ✓ Juice of 1 lime
- ✓ Salt and pepper, to taste
- ✓ Lime wedges for serving

COOKING STEPS

1. Toss the prawns with olive oil, chili flakes, oregano, lime juice, salt, and pepper.
2. Preheat the Air Fryer to 200°C (392°F).
3. Place the prawns in the Air Fryer basket in a single layer.
4. Cook for 8 minutes, turning halfway, until they are pink and slightly charred.
5. Serve with additional lime wedges.

NUTRITIONAL FACTS: (PER SERVING)

- ❖ Calories: 200 kcal
- ❖ Protein: 20g
- ❖ Fat: 12g
- ❖ Carbohydrates: 2g

FINAL WORD

This Grilled Fresh Spicy Prawns with Lime and Oregano recipe is a delightful way to enjoy seafood with a spicy twist. The Air Fryer ensures the prawns are perfectly cooked, offering a juicy, flavorful bite each time. Perfect for a quick lunch or a fancy dinner, this dish will tantalize your taste buds and leave you craving more.

Recipe-17: Halibut With Hazelnut Crust With Roast Red Pepper Sauce

Medium | **Cooking: 20 Mins** | **Servings: 01** | **Prep: 20 Mins**

INTRODUCTION

Indulge in the culinary delight of "Halibut with Hazelnut Crust and Roast Red Pepper Sauce, Asparagus, Cauliflower, and Shiitake Mushrooms," a sophisticated Air Fryer fish recipe. This dish combines the delicate flavor of halibut with a nutty hazelnut crust, complemented by a tangy roast red pepper sauce and a medley of roasted vegetables. Perfect for those seeking a gourmet, nutritious meal with a symphony of flavors.

INGREDIENTS

- ✓ 1 halibut fillet
- ✓ 1/4 cup ground hazelnuts
- ✓ 1/2 cup asparagus, trimmed
- ✓ 1/2 cup cauliflower florets
- ✓ 1/4 cup shiitake mushrooms, sliced
- ✓ 2 tbsp roast red pepper sauce
- ✓ Salt and pepper, to taste
- ✓ Olive oil for brushing

COOKING STEPS

1. Preheat the Air Fryer to 200°C (392°F).
2. Season the halibut with salt and pepper and brush with olive oil.
3. Coat the fillet with ground hazelnuts.
4. Place the halibut, asparagus, cauliflower, and mushrooms in the Air Fryer basket.
5. Cook for 20 minutes or until the fish is cooked and the vegetables are tender.
6. Serve the halibut with the roasted vegetables and roast red pepper sauce.

NUTRITIONAL FACTS: (PER SERVING)

- ❖ Calories: 420 kcal
- ❖ Protein: 35g
- ❖ Fat: 24g
- ❖ Carbohydrates: 20g

FINAL WORD

This Halibut with Hazelnut Crust and Roast Red Pepper Sauce, accompanied by asparagus, cauliflower, and shiitake mushrooms, is a harmonious blend of flavors and textures. The Air Fryer technique offers a healthier way to enjoy a rich, flavorful meal. Whether for a special occasion or a sophisticated weeknight dinner, this recipe will impress and satisfy you.

Recipe-18: Red Curry With Salmon In Coconut Milk Sauce

Easy | **Cooking:15 Mins** | **Servings: 01** | **Prep:10 Mins**

INTRODUCTION

Embark on a flavorful journey with "Red Curry with Salmon in Coconut Milk Sauce," an enticing Air Fryer fish recipe that melds the rich, aromatic red curry spices with coconut milk's creamy sweetness. This dish features succulent salmon fillets immersed in a luscious sauce, offering an exotic and comforting culinary experience, perfect for those who cherish the fusion of traditional and contemporary flavors.

INGREDIENTS

- ✓ 1 salmon fillet
- ✓ 2 tbsp red curry paste
- ✓ 1/2 cup coconut milk
- ✓ 1/2 tsp fish sauce
- ✓ 1/2 tsp brown sugar
- ✓ 1/4 cup bell pepper, sliced
- ✓ 1/4 cup bamboo shoots
- ✓ Fresh basil leaves for garnish
- ✓ Salt, to taste

COOKING STEPS

1. Preheat the Air Fryer to 180°C (356°F).
2. Season the salmon fillet with salt.
3. Mix a bowl of red curry paste, coconut milk, fish sauce, and brown sugar.
4. Place the salmon in the Air Fryer basket.
5. Pour the curry mixture over the salmon.
6. Add bell pepper and bamboo shoots around the salmon.
7. Cook for 15 minutes or until the salmon is cooked through.
8. Garnish with fresh basil leaves before serving.

NUTRITIONAL FACTS: (PER SERVING)

- ❖ Calories: 450 kcal
- ❖ Protein: 25g
- ❖ Fat: 35g
- ❖ Carbohydrates: 10g

FINAL WORD

In conclusion, this Red Curry with Salmon in Coconut Milk Sauce recipe is a delightful blend of rich flavors and textures, bringing a touch of Thai cuisine to your dining table. The Air Fryer ensures a healthy cooking method, infusing the salmon with the aromatic curry while maintaining moisture. Perfect for a cozy dinner or a special occasion, this dish promises a satisfying and exotic culinary experience.

Recipe-19: Trout With Crispy Almond Crust And Baked Mashed Potatoes

Medium | **Cooking: 30 Mins** | **Servings: 01** | **Prep: 20 Mins**

INTRODUCTION

Savor the delightful fusion of textures in "Trout with Crispy Almond Crust and Baked Mashed Potatoes," a sumptuous Air Fryer fish recipe. This dish pairs the delicate flavor of trout with a crunchy almond topping alongside smooth, creamy mashed potatoes, baked to perfection. Ideal for those seeking a comforting yet sophisticated meal, it's a harmonious blend of rustic charm and refined taste.

INGREDIENTS

- 1 trout fillet
- 1/4 cup ground almonds
- 1 cup mashed potatoes
- 1 tbsp butter
- 1/2 tsp garlic powder
- Salt and pepper, to taste
- Fresh parsley for garnish

COOKING STEPS

1. Preheat the Air Fryer to 180°C (356°F).
2. Season the trout fillet with salt, pepper, and garlic powder.
3. Coat the fillet with ground almonds.
4. Place the trout in the Air Fryer basket.
5. Mix mashed potatoes with butter in a separate dish, then place alongside the trout.
6. Cook for 30 minutes or until the trout is cooked and the crust golden.
7. Garnish with fresh parsley before serving.

NUTRITIONAL FACTS: (PER SERVING)

- Calories: 550 kcal
- Protein: 30g
- Fat: 35g
- Carbohydrates: 35g

FINAL WORD

This Trout with Crispy Almond Crust and Baked Mashed Potatoes recipe offers an exquisite dining experience. The Air Fryer brings out the best in both the fish and the potatoes, ensuring a nutritious and indulgent meal. Perfect for those special occasions or when you're in the mood for something extra special, this dish is sure to delight and satisfy.

Recipe-20: Roasted Swordfish With Leek Ginger And Sesame Seed

Easy | **Cooking: 15 Mins** | **Servings: 01** | **Prep: 10 Mins**

INTRODUCTION

Embark on a culinary adventure with "Roasted Swordfish with Leek, Ginger, and Sesame Seed," a delectable Air Fryer fish recipe. This dish features the robust flavor of swordfish, enhanced with the subtle sharpness of leek, ginger warmth, and sesame seeds' nuttiness. Ideal for those seeking a sophisticated yet simple seafood meal, it's a perfect blend of distinct flavors and textures.

INGREDIENTS

- ✓ 1 swordfish steak
- ✓ 1/4 cup leeks, finely sliced
- ✓ 1 tsp ginger, grated
- ✓ 1 tbsp sesame seeds
- ✓ 1 tbsp olive oil
- ✓ Salt and pepper, to taste

COOKING STEPS

1. Preheat the Air Fryer to 200°C (392°F).
2. Season the swordfish steak with salt and pepper.
3. Mix leeks, ginger, and sesame seeds with olive oil.
4. Top the swordfish with the leek mixture.
5. Place the fish in the Air Fryer basket.
6. Cook for 15 minutes or until the swordfish is cooked and the topping is golden.

NUTRITIONAL FACTS: (PER SERVING)

- ❖ Calories: 300 kcal
- ❖ Fat: 18g
- ❖ Protein: 25g
- ❖ Carbohydrates: 5g

FINAL WORD

In conclusion, this Roasted Swordfish with Leek, Ginger, and Sesame Seed recipe is a delightful way to enjoy a unique fish variety. The Air Fryer ensures a healthy cooking process, keeping the fish moist while crisping the topping. This dish is sure to impress with its balance of flavors and ease of preparation, perfect for a special dinner or a nutritious everyday meal.

Chapter-03: Meat Recipes

Recipe-21: Juicy Sliced Beef Ribeye Steak

Easy | **Cooking: 15 Mins** | **Servings: 01** | **Prep: 10 Mins**

INTRODUCTION

Welcome to this mouth-watering recipe for a juicy sliced beef ribeye steak cooked ideally using an Air Fryer. This dish is a perfect blend of simplicity and flavor, making it an ideal choice for anyone who enjoys a gourmet meal at home. Whether cooking for yourself or impressing guests, this recipe will surely delight you.

INGREDIENTS

- ✓ 1 large beef ribeye steak (about 1-inch thick)
- ✓ 1 tablespoon olive oil
- ✓ 1 teaspoon coarse salt
- ✓ ½ teaspoon freshly ground black pepper
- ✓ 1 teaspoon garlic powder
- ✓ 1 sprig of fresh rosemary (optional)

COOKING STEPS

1. Preheat your Air Fryer to 400°F (200°C).
2. Rub the steak with olive oil and season it with salt, pepper, and garlic powder.
3. Place the steak in the Air Fryer basket and cook for about 7-8 minutes for medium-rare, or adjust according to your preferred level of doneness.
4. Halfway through, flip the steak and add a sprig of rosemary for added flavor.
5. Once cooked, let the steak rest for 5 minutes before slicing to ensure juiciness.

NUTRITIONAL FACTS: (PER SERVING)

- ❖ Calories: 650
- ❖ Protein: 47g
- ❖ Fat: 48g
- ❖ Carbohydrates: 0g
- ❖ Sodium: 620mg
- ❖ Cholesterol: 135mg

FINAL WORD

In conclusion, this Air Fryer ribeye steak recipe offers a quick and easy way to enjoy a juicy, flavorful steak. It's perfect for a busy weeknight dinner or a special occasion. Serve with your favorite side dishes and enjoy the tender, succulent flavors of a perfectly cooked ribeye steak. Bon Appétit!

Recipe-22: Roasted Beef Steak Striploin Juicy Mustard Sauce

Medium   **Cooking: 20 Mins**   **Servings: 01**   **Prep: 15 Mins**

INTRODUCTION

Dive into culinary delights with this succulent Roasted Beef Steak Striploin bathed in rich, tangy mustard sauce. This recipe, prepared in an Air Fryer, combines the robust flavors of beef with the zesty kick of mustard, creating a dish that's both easy to make and a joy to eat. Perfect for meat lovers looking for a gourmet experience right at home.

pg. 48

INGREDIENTS

- ✓ 1 beef striploin steak (about 1-inch thick)
- ✓ 2 tablespoons Dijon mustard
- ✓ 1 tablespoon olive oil
- ✓ 1 teaspoon honey
- ✓ ½ teaspoon garlic powder
- ✓ Salt and freshly ground black pepper to taste
- ✓ Fresh herbs for garnish (such as thyme or parsley)

COOKING STEPS

1. Preheat the Air Fryer to 390°F (200°C).
2. Mix Dijon mustard, honey, olive oil, garlic powder, salt, and pepper in a bowl to create the sauce.
3. Coat the steak evenly with half of the mustard sauce.
4. Place the steak in the Air Fryer and cook for 10 minutes, then flip and cook for 10 minutes for a medium-rare finish. Adjust cooking time for desired doneness.
5. Let the steak rest for 5 minutes, then slice and drizzle with the remaining mustard sauce.

NUTRITIONAL FACTS: (PER SERVING)

- ❖ Calories: 480
- ❖ Protein: 38g
- ❖ Fat: 34g
- ❖ Carbohydrates: 4g
- ❖ Sodium: 400mg
- ❖ Cholesterol: 90mg

FINAL WORD

To wrap up, this Roasted Beef Steak Striploin with Juicy Mustard Sauce is a dish that promises to tantalize your taste buds. It's a perfect blend of tender beef and bold mustard flavors, all made effortlessly in an Air Fryer. Ideal for a special dinner or a satisfying meal, this dish is sure to impress both you and your guests. Enjoy your culinary creation!

Recipe-23: Grilled Lamb Mutton Meat Chops Steaks

Medium | **Cooking:15 Mins** | **Servings: 01** | **Prep:20 Mins**

INTRODUCTION

Savor the rich and distinctive flavors of Grilled Lamb Mutton Meat Chops, a delectable dish that brings the essence of traditional grilling to the convenience of your kitchen with an Air Fryer. These lamb chops, seasoned to perfection, offer a tender, juicy treat bound to satisfy your craving for a hearty and flavorful meal, perfect for any meat lover's dining table.

INGREDIENTS

- ✓ 2 lamb mutton chops
- ✓ 1 tablespoon olive oil
- ✓ 1 teaspoon rosemary, finely chopped
- ✓ 1 garlic clove, minced
- ✓ Salt and freshly ground black pepper to taste
- ✓ 1/2 teaspoon paprika
- ✓ 1/4 teaspoon cumin

COOKING STEPS

1. Preheat the Air Fryer to 400°F (200°C).
2. Mix olive oil, rosemary, garlic, salt, pepper, paprika, and cumin in a small bowl.
3. Rub the mixture evenly over both sides of the lamb chops.
4. Place the chops in the Air Fryer basket, ensuring they are not overlapping.
5. Cook for 7-8 minutes, then flip and cook for another 7-8 minutes for medium-rare, or adjust based on your preferred level of doneness.
6. Let the chops rest for a few minutes before serving.

NUTRITIONAL FACTS: (PER SERVING)

- ❖ Calories: 340
- ❖ Protein: 28g
- ❖ Fat: 24g
- ❖ Carbohydrates: 1g
- ❖ Sodium: 75mg
- ❖ Cholesterol: 85mg

FINAL WORD

In conclusion, these Grilled Lamb Mutton Meat Chops offer a delightful fusion of tenderness and robust flavors; all made easy and convenient with an Air Fryer. Whether you want to impress guests or treat yourself to a gourmet meal, this recipe promises a memorable dining experience. Pair it with your favorite sides and enjoy a delicious, hearty meal.

Recipe-24: Bacon Wrapped Sirloin Steak With Herbs

Intermediate | **Cooking: 20 Mins** | **Servings: 01** | **Prep: 15 Mins**

INTRODUCTION

Embark on a culinary journey with this Bacon Wrapped Sirloin Steak with Herbs, a recipe that elevates the classic steak to new heights. Combining the savoriness of bacon with the robust flavors of sirloin and a bouquet of herbs, this dish is a symphony of tastes and textures. Prepared in an Air Fryer, it's a perfect recipe for those seeking a gourmet experience at home with minimal fuss.

INGREDIENTS

- ✓ 1 sirloin steak (about 8 oz)
- ✓ 2 strips of bacon
- ✓ 1 teaspoon fresh thyme, chopped
- ✓ 1 teaspoon fresh rosemary, chopped
- ✓ Salt and freshly ground black pepper to taste
- ✓ 1 tablespoon olive oil

COOKING STEPS

1. Preheat the Air Fryer to 390°F (200°C).
2. Season the sirloin steak with salt, pepper, thyme, and rosemary.
3. Wrap the steak with the bacon strips, securing them with toothpicks if necessary.
4. Brush the steak with olive oil.
5. Place the steak in the Air Fryer basket and cook for 10 minutes, then flip and cook for 10 minutes, or until the bacon is crispy and the steak reaches your desired level of doneness.
6. Let the steak rest for 5 minutes before serving.

NUTRITIONAL FACTS: (PER SERVING)

- ❖ Calories: 540
- ❖ Protein: 48g
- ❖ Fat: 36g
- ❖ Carbohydrates: 0g
- ❖ Sodium: 760mg
- ❖ Cholesterol: 130mg

FINAL WORD

As a finale, this Bacon Wrapped Sirloin Steak with Herbs is not just a meal; it's an experience. The combination of juicy steak and crispy bacon, all infused with the aromatic flavors of fresh herbs, creates an indulgent and satisfying dish. Perfect for a special occasion or a treat-yourself night, this recipe is sure to impress and delight your taste buds.

Recipe-25: Korean Bulgogi Beef

Easy | **Cooking: 10 Mins** | **Servings: 01** | **Prep: 30 Mins**

INTRODUCTION

Immerse yourself in the flavors of Korea with this exquisite Korean Bulgogi Beef recipe, a traditional dish that marries sweet and savory in every bite. Made in the convenience of an Air Fryer, this dish brings the authentic taste of Korean cuisine to your kitchen. Ideal for anyone seeking to explore international flavors, this Bulgogi Beef is not just a meal; it's a cultural experience.

INGREDIENTS

- ✓ 200g thinly sliced beef (sirloin or ribeye)
- ✓ 2 tablespoons soy sauce
- ✓ 1 tablespoon brown sugar
- ✓ 1 tablespoon sesame oil
- ✓ 2 cloves garlic, minced
- ✓ 1/2 small pear, grated
- ✓ 1 tablespoon finely chopped green onion
- ✓ 1/2 teaspoon ground black pepper
- ✓ 1 teaspoon sesame seeds

COOKING STEPS

1. Combine the marinade in a bowl with soy sauce, brown sugar, sesame oil, garlic, grated pear, green onion, and black pepper.
2. Add the beef to the marinade, ensuring each slice is well coated. Marinate for at least 20 minutes.
3. Preheat the Air Fryer to 390°F (200°C).
4. Place the marinated beef in the Air Fryer basket in a single layer. Cook for about 5 minutes, then stir and cook for another 5 minutes until the meat is cooked and slightly caramelized.
5. Sprinkle sesame seeds over the cooked beef before serving.

NUTRITIONAL FACTS: (PER SERVING)

- ❖ Calories: 310
- ❖ Protein: 24g
- ❖ Fat: 18g
- ❖ Carbohydrates: 12g
- ❖ Sodium: 970mg
- ❖ Cholesterol: 60mg

FINAL WORD

To conclude, Korean Bulgogi Beef is a delightful dish that brings a taste of Korea to your dining table. This recipe's perfect blend of sweet, savory, and umami flavors makes it an ideal choice for a quick yet exotic meal. Serve it with steamed rice or lettuce wraps for a complete and satisfying experience. Enjoy the journey of flavors!

Recipe-26: Boneless Pork Chops BBQ

Easy | **Cooking:12 Mins** | **Servings: 01** | **Prep:10 Mins**

INTRODUCTION

Indulge in the mouthwatering world of BBQ with these boneless pork chops seasoned with a blend of savory spices. This Air Fryer recipe transforms simple pork chops into a BBQ masterpiece, offering a delightful balance of smoky and sweet flavors. It's an ideal dish for those who crave the taste of outdoor grilling with the ease and convenience of indoor cooking.

INGREDIENTS

- ✓ 1 boneless pork chop (about 1-inch thick)
- ✓ 1 tablespoon BBQ seasoning
- ✓ 1 teaspoon olive oil
- ✓ Salt and freshly ground black pepper to taste

COOKING STEPS

1. Preheat the Air Fryer to 375°F (190°C).
2. Rub the pork chop with olive oil, then season generously with BBQ seasoning, salt, and pepper.
3. Place the pork chop in the Air Fryer basket.
4. Cook for 6 minutes, flip the pork chop, and cook for 6 minutes until it reaches an internal temperature of 145°F (63°C).
5. Let the pork chop rest for a few minutes before serving.

NUTRITIONAL FACTS: (PER SERVING)

- ❖ Calories: 220
- ❖ Protein: 23g
- ❖ Fat: 12g
- ❖ Carbohydrates: 0g
- ❖ Sodium: 500mg
- ❖ Cholesterol: 65mg

FINAL WORD

In summary, these boneless pork chops BBQ seasoned are a testament to the magic of simple ingredients and the right seasonings. Whether you're looking to spice up your weekday dinner routine or impress at your next gathering, this Air Fryer recipe is a surefire way to delight your palate with minimal effort. Enjoy the rich BBQ flavors in every tender bite.

Recipe-27: Garlic Butter Steak Bites

Easy | **Cooking: 08 Mins** | **Servings: 01** | **Prep: 10 Mins**

INTRODUCTION

Experience the delectable combination of garlic and butter in this tantalizing Garlic Butter Steak Bite recipe. Prepared in an Air Fryer, these juicy, flavorful bites are a perfect quick and easy dish that doesn't compromise taste. Ideal for steak lovers who appreciate a garlicky twist, this dish is a great way to enjoy a gourmet steak experience in bite-sized form.

INGREDIENTS

- ✓ 200g sirloin steak, cut into 1-inch cubes
- ✓ 2 tablespoons butter, melted
- ✓ 2 cloves garlic, minced
- ✓ Salt and freshly ground black pepper to taste
- ✓ 1/2 teaspoon dried parsley (or fresh, chopped)

COOKING STEPS

1. Preheat the Air Fryer to 400°F (200°C).
2. Mix the steak cubes with melted butter, garlic, salt, and pepper in a bowl.
3. Place the steak bites in the Air Fryer basket in a single layer.
4. Cook for 4 minutes, shake the basket or turn the steak bites, and cook for another 4 minutes or until they reach your desired level of doneness.
5. Sprinkle with parsley before serving.

NUTRITIONAL FACTS: (PER SERVING)

- ❖ Calories: 320
- ❖ Protein: 26g
- ❖ Fat: 23g
- ❖ Carbohydrates: 1g
- ❖ Sodium: 200mg
- ❖ Cholesterol: 80mg

FINAL WORD

To wrap it up, these Garlic Butter Steak Bites are a fantastic way to enjoy the rich steak flavors with the aromatic punch of garlic. They're perfect for a quick dinner, a party appetizer, or a savory snack. Simple, speedy, and scrumptious, this Air Fryer dish will become a fast favorite in your recipe collection.

Recipe-28: Freshly Honey Maple Glazed Ham

Easy | **Cooking: 20 Mins** | **Servings: 01** | **Prep: 15 Mins**

INTRODUCTION

Delight in the sweet and savory fusion of this Freshly Honey Maple Glazed Ham, a dish that effortlessly brings a touch of elegance to your dining table. Crafted in an Air Fryer, this recipe perfectly blends honey's sweetness and maple's rich flavor, enveloping the tender ham in a luscious glaze. It's ideal for those seeking a gourmet twist on classic ham.

INGREDIENTS

- ✓ 1 slice of ham (about 200g)
- ✓ 2 tablespoons honey
- ✓ 1 tablespoon maple syrup
- ✓ 1 teaspoon Dijon mustard
- ✓ 1/2 teaspoon apple cider vinegar
- ✓ Pinch of ground cloves
- ✓ Pinch of ground cinnamon

COOKING STEPS

1. Preheat the Air Fryer to 350°F (175°C).
2. Mix honey, maple syrup, Dijon mustard, apple cider vinegar, cloves, and cinnamon in a small bowl to make the glaze.
3. Brush the ham slice generously with the glaze on both sides.
4. Place the ham in the Air Fryer basket and cook for 10 minutes.
5. Open the Air Fryer, apply another layer of glaze to the ham, and cook for 10 minutes or until the edges start caramelizing.

NUTRITIONAL FACTS: (PER SERVING)

- ❖ Calories: 320
- ❖ Protein: 25g
- ❖ Fat: 10g
- ❖ Carbohydrates: 35g
- ❖ Sodium: 1420mg
- ❖ Cholesterol: 60mg

FINAL WORD

This Freshly Honey Maple Glazed Ham offers a delightful twist to traditional ham dishes. With its rich glaze and the unique texture that the Air Fryer provides, this dish is a joy to prepare and a treat to the palate. Perfect for a festive meal or a special weekend treat, it's sure to be a crowd-pleaser.

Recipe-29: Chipotle Grilled Flank Steak

Easy | **Cooking:10 Mins** | **Servings: 01** | **Prep:25 Mins**

INTRODUCTION

Embark on a flavorful adventure with this Chipotle Grilled Flank Steak, which perfectly marries Chipotle's smokiness with the flank steak's tenderness. This Air Fryer recipe offers an easy and efficient way to enjoy grilled steak's rich, bold flavors with a spicy twist. It's an excellent choice for anyone who loves a bit of heat with their meat.

INGREDIENTS

- ✓ 1 flank steak (about 200g)
- ✓ 1 tablespoon chipotle in adobo sauce, finely chopped
- ✓ 1 tablespoon olive oil
- ✓ 1 garlic clove, minced
- ✓ 1/2 teaspoon cumin
- ✓ Salt and freshly ground black pepper to taste

COOKING STEPS

1. Combine the marinade with Chipotle, olive oil, garlic, cumin, salt, and pepper in a bowl.
2. Coat the flank steak evenly with the marinade and let it rest for at least 20 minutes.
3. Preheat the Air Fryer to 400°F (200°C).
4. Place the marinated steak in the Air Fryer basket and cook for 5 minutes. Flip the steak and cook for another 5 minutes for medium-rare, or adjust according to your preference.
5. Let the steak rest for a few minutes before slicing against the grain.

NUTRITIONAL FACTS: (PER SERVING)

- ❖ Calories: 310
- ❖ Protein: 24g
- ❖ Fat: 22g
- ❖ Carbohydrates: 2g
- ❖ Sodium: 500mg
- ❖ Cholesterol: 60m

FINAL WORD

In conclusion, this Chipotle Grilled Flank Steak is a vibrant and flavor-packed dish that satisfies your craving for something spicy and meaty. Whether looking for a quick weeknight dinner or a special weekend treat, this Air Fryer recipe is a foolproof way to enjoy a delicious, restaurant-quality steak at home.

Recipe-30: Honey Mustard Chicken Thighs With Herbs

Medium | **Cooking:10 Mins** | **Servings: 01** | **Prep:25 Mins**

INTRODUCTION

Embark on a flavorful adventure with this Chipotle Grilled Flank Steak, which perfectly marries Chipotle's smokiness with the flank steak's tenderness. This Air Fryer recipe offers an easy and efficient way to enjoy grilled steak's rich, bold flavors with a spicy twist. It's an excellent choice for anyone who loves a bit of heat with their meat.

INGREDIENTS

- ✓ 1 flank steak (about 200g)
- ✓ 1 tablespoon chipotle in adobo sauce, finely chopped
- ✓ 1 tablespoon olive oil
- ✓ 1 garlic clove, minced
- ✓ 1/2 teaspoon cumin
- ✓ Salt and freshly ground black pepper to taste

COOKING STEPS

1. Combine the marinade with Chipotle, olive oil, garlic, cumin, salt, and pepper in a bowl.
2. Coat the flank steak evenly with the marinade and let it rest for at least 20 minutes.
3. Preheat the Air Fryer to 400°F (200°C).
4. Place the marinated steak in the Air Fryer basket and cook for 5 minutes. Flip the steak and cook for another 5 minutes for medium-rare, or adjust according to your preference.
5. Let the steak rest for a few minutes before slicing against the grain.

NUTRITIONAL FACTS: (PER SERVING)

- ❖ Calories: 310
- ❖ Protein: 24g
- ❖ Fat: 22g
- ❖ Carbohydrates: 2g
- ❖ Sodium: 500mg
- ❖ Cholesterol: 60mg

FINAL WORD

In conclusion, this Chipotle Grilled Flank Steak is a vibrant and flavor-packed dish that satisfies your craving for something spicy and meaty. Whether looking for a quick weeknight dinner or a special weekend treat, this Air Fryer recipe is a foolproof way to enjoy a delicious, restaurant-quality steak at home.

Chapter-04: Seafood Recipes

Recipe-31: Crispy Calamari Rings With Lemon Wedge

Easy | **Cooking: 08 Mins** | **Servings: 01** | **Prep: 15 Mins**

INTRODUCTION

Indulge in the classic and ever-popular delight of Crispy Calamari Rings, complemented with a zesty lemon wedge. This Air Fryer seafood recipe offers a lighter alternative to traditional frying, delivering the same crispy texture and tantalizing flavor. Perfect for seafood lovers and those seeking a simple yet satisfying appetizer or meal, this dish is a testament to the versatility of the Air Fryer.

INGREDIENTS

- ✓ 150g calamari rings
- ✓ 1/2 cup all-purpose flour
- ✓ 1 teaspoon paprika
- ✓ 1/2 teaspoon garlic powder
- ✓ Salt and freshly ground black pepper to taste
- ✓ 1 egg, beaten
- ✓ 1 lemon wedge for serving

COOKING STEPS

1. Mix flour, paprika, garlic powder, salt, and pepper in a bowl.
2. Dip calamari rings in the beaten egg, then coat with flour.
3. Preheat the Air Fryer to 400°F (200°C).
4. Arrange the calamari rings in a single layer in the Air Fryer basket.
5. Cook for 4 minutes, flip the rings, then cook for another 4 minutes until golden and crispy.
6. Serve with a lemon wedge on the side.

NUTRITIONAL FACTS: (PER SERVING)

- ❖ Calories: 300
- ❖ Protein: 18g
- ❖ Fat: 5g
- ❖ Carbohydrates: 38g
- ❖ Sodium: 300mg
- ❖ Cholesterol: 220mg

FINAL WORD

In conclusion, these Crispy Calamari Rings with Lemon Wedges are a delightful way to enjoy a seafood favorite with less guilt. Whether as a starter, a snack, or a main course, this Air Fryer recipe is a crowd-pleaser, offering a crispy, flavorful treat that's as enjoyable to make as it is to eat. Squeeze some lemon on top for that extra zest, and savor each bite!

Recipe-32: Stir-Fried Lobster With Butter & Garlic Sauce

Medium   **Cooking:10 Mins**   **Servings: 01**   **Prep:20 Mins**

INTRODUCTION

Dive into the luxurious taste of Stir-fried Lobster with Butter and garlic Sauce, a decadent Air Fryer seafood recipe that brings the elegance of gourmet dining into your home. This dish beautifully combines the richness of butter and the aromatic allure of garlic, enveloping the tender lobster in a sumptuous sauce. It's a splendid choice for a special occasion or when you want to treat yourself to something truly exquisite.

INGREDIENTS

- ✓ 1 lobster tail, split and cleaned
- ✓ 2 tablespoons butter, melted
- ✓ 2 cloves garlic, minced
- ✓ 1 teaspoon lemon juice
- ✓ Salt and freshly ground black pepper to taste
- ✓ Fresh parsley, chopped for garnish

COOKING STEPS

1. Preheat the Air Fryer to 380°F (190°C).
2. Mix melted butter, garlic, lemon juice, salt, and pepper in a bowl.
3. Brush the lobster tail with the garlic butter sauce.
4. Place the lobster tail in the Air Fryer basket.
5. Cook for 8-10 minutes or until the lobster is cooked through and slightly golden.
6. Garnish with chopped parsley before serving.

NUTRITIONAL FACTS: (PER SERVING)

- ❖ Calories: 230
- ❖ Protein: 22g
- ❖ Fat: 14g
- ❖ Carbohydrates: 2g
- ❖ Sodium: 490mg
- ❖ Cholesterol: 60mg

FINAL WORD

This Stir-fried Lobster with Butter and garlic Sauce is an indulgence worth savoring. Combining buttery garlic sauce and perfectly cooked lobster creates a dish that's not just a meal but an experience. Whether for a romantic dinner or a special treat, this Air Fryer recipe will impress and satisfy your seafood cravings.

Recipe-33: Fried Coconut Shrimp On A Skewer With A Dipping Sauce

Easy   **Cooking:10 Mins**   **Servings: 01**   **Prep:15 Mins**

INTRODUCTION

Embark on a tropical culinary adventure with Fried Coconut Shrimp on a Skewer, accompanied by a tantalizing dipping sauce. This Air Fryer seafood recipe offers a delightful combination of crispy coconut coating and succulent shrimp, making it a perfect appetizer or main dish. Ideal for those who enjoy a hint of sweetness and crunch in their seafood, this dish is a breeze to prepare and a joy to devour.

INGREDIENTS

- ✓ 6 large shrimp, peeled and deveined
- ✓ 1/4 cup shredded coconut
- ✓ 1/4 cup breadcrumbs
- ✓ 1 egg, beaten
- ✓ Salt and pepper, to taste
- ✓ Wooden skewers
- ✓ Your choice of dipping sauce

COOKING STEPS

1. Preheat the Air Fryer to 400°F (200°C).
2. Season the shrimp with salt and pepper.
3. Dip each shrimp in the beaten egg, then coat it with shredded coconut and breadcrumbs.
4. Carefully thread the coated shrimp onto skewers.
5. Place the shrimp skewers in the Air Fryer basket and cook for 5 minutes. Flip the skewers and cook for another 5 minutes until the shrimp are golden and crispy.
6. Serve with your favorite dipping sauce.

NUTRITIONAL FACTS: (PER SERVING)

- ❖ Calories: 310
- ❖ Protein: 15g
- ❖ Fat: 15g
- ❖ Carbohydrates: 26g
- ❖ Sodium: 370mg
- ❖ Cholesterol: 185mg

FINAL WORD

To conclude, these Fried Coconut Shrimp on a Skewer are a delightful way to bring a taste of the tropics to your table. The combination of crunchy coconut and tender shrimp, all made effortlessly in the Air Fryer, creates a dish that's visually appealing and packed with flavor. Enjoy this easy-to-make, exotic treat that's perfect for any occasion.

Recipe-34: Fish Beer Batter And Chips With Green Pea And Tartar Sauce

Medium | **Cooking: 25 Mins** | **Servings: 01** | **Prep: 20 Mins**

INTRODUCTION

Indulge in a classic favorite with a twist in this Fish Beer Batter and Chips recipe, complemented by green pea and tartar sauce. This Air Fryer seafood dish reimagines the beloved fish and chips, offering a crispy, golden treat with less oil. Perfect for those who cherish traditional flavors with a modern, healthier approach, this recipe promises a satisfying meal with a delightful crunch.

INGREDIENTS

- ✓ 1 fish fillet (cod or haddock preferred)
- ✓ 1/2 cup all-purpose flour
- ✓ 1/2 cup beer
- ✓ 1/2 teaspoon baking powder
- ✓ 1 large potato, cut into chips
- ✓ 1/2 cup green peas
- ✓ Salt and pepper, to taste
- ✓ Tartar sauce for serving

COOKING STEPS

1. Mix flour, beer, and baking powder in a bowl to create a smooth batter. Season with salt and pepper.
2. Dip the fish fillet into the batter, ensuring it's well coated.
3. Preheat the Air Fryer to 360°F (180°C).
4. Place the battered fish in the Air Fryer basket. Cook for 12-15 minutes until golden and crispy.
5. Season with salt and pepper for the chips, and cook in the Air Fryer for 20 minutes, shaking halfway through.
6. Boil green peas until tender, drain, and season with salt and pepper.
7. Serve the fish and chips with green peas and tartar sauce.

NUTRITIONAL FACTS: (PER SERVING)

- ❖ Calories: 600
- ❖ Protein: 28g
- ❖ Fat: 15g
- ❖ Carbohydrates: 85g
- ❖ Sodium: 700mg
- ❖ Cholesterol: 50mg

FINAL WORD

This Fish Beer Batter and Chips with Green Pea and Tartar Sauce is a delightful reinvention of a beloved classic. The Air Fryer brings a new level of healthiness and ease to this dish, ensuring a crispy texture without the heaviness of oil. Perfect for a cozy night in or a casual dinner, this recipe is sure to please seafood and comfort food enthusiasts alike.

Recipe-35: Homemade Maryland Crab Cakes

Medium | **Cooking: 10 Mins** | **Servings: 01** | **Prep: 20 Mins**

INTRODUCTION

Delve into the savory world of Maryland Crab Cakes, a classic seafood dish that captures the essence of coastal cuisine. This Air Fryer version offers a healthier take on the traditional recipe, delivering the same delicious flavors and textures with less oil. Perfect for crab lovers and those seeking a taste of the East Coast, these crab cakes are sure to tantalize your taste buds with every bite.

INGREDIENTS

- ✓ 1/2 cup lump crab meat
- ✓ 1/4 cup breadcrumbs
- ✓ 1 egg, beaten
- ✓ 1 tablespoon mayonnaise
- ✓ 1 teaspoon Dijon mustard
- ✓ 1/2 teaspoon Old Bay seasoning
- ✓ 1/4 teaspoon Worcestershire sauce
- ✓ Lemon wedges for serving

COOKING STEPS

1. Mix crab meat, breadcrumbs, egg, mayonnaise, Dijon mustard, Old Bay seasoning, and Worcestershire sauce in a bowl.
2. Form the mixture into small patties.
3. Preheat the Air Fryer to 370°F (190°C).
4. Place the crab cakes in the Air Fryer basket and cook for 5 minutes. Flip the crab cakes and cook for 5 minutes until golden and crispy.
5. Serve with lemon wedges on the side.

NUTRITIONAL FACTS: (PER SERVING)

- ❖ Calories: 290
- ❖ Protein: 20g
- ❖ Fat: 15g
- ❖ Carbohydrates: 18g
- ❖ Sodium: 610mg
- ❖ Cholesterol: 140mg

FINAL WORD

In conclusion, these Maryland Crab Cakes are a delightful treat, perfect for any seafood enthusiast looking to enjoy a classic dish more healthily. The Air Fryer brings out the best in these cakes, ensuring a crispy exterior and a moist, flavorful interior. These crab cakes will impress as an appetizer or a main dish.

Recipe-36: Scalloped Lemon Garlic Butter Sauce Grilled

Easy **Cooking: 06 Mins** **Servings: 01** **Prep: 10 Mins**

INTRODUCTION

Savor the exquisite blend of flavors in this Scalloped Lemon Garlic Butter Sauce Grilled dish, a luxurious seafood recipe crafted in the Air Fryer. This dish combines the delicate taste of scallops with a rich, zesty lemon garlic butter sauce, creating an elegant and flavorful experience. Perfect for seafood connoisseurs and anyone looking to add a gourmet touch to their meal repertoire.

pg. 76

INGREDIENTS

- ✓ 4 large scallops
- ✓ 2 tablespoons butter
- ✓ 1 garlic clove, minced
- ✓ 1 tablespoon lemon juice
- ✓ Salt and freshly ground black pepper to taste
- ✓ Fresh parsley, chopped for garnish

COOKING STEPS

1. Preheat the Air Fryer to 390°F (200°C).
2. In a small saucepan, melt butter over medium heat. Add garlic and cook until fragrant. Remove from heat and stir in lemon juice.
3. Season the scallops with salt and pepper.
4. Place the scallops in the Air Fryer basket and cook for 3 minutes.
5. Flip the scallops, then cook for 3 minutes or until opaque and slightly golden.
6. Drizzle the lemon garlic butter sauce over the scallops and garnish with parsley.

NUTRITIONAL FACTS: (PER SERVING)

- ❖ Calories: 230
- ❖ Protein: 14g
- ❖ Fat: 18g
- ❖ Carbohydrates: 4g
- ❖ Sodium: 380mg
- ❖ Cholesterol: 41mg

FINAL WORD

To wrap up, this Scalloped Lemon Garlic Butter Sauce Grilled dish is a simple yet elegant seafood delight sure to impress. The Air Fryer ensures the scallops are perfectly cooked, while the lemon garlic butter sauce adds a rich and flavorful dimension. It's an ideal recipe for a special occasion or when you want to treat yourself to a luxurious meal.

Recipe-37: Bang Bang Shrimps

Easy | **Cooking: 08 Mins** | **Servings: 01** | **Prep: 15 Mins**

INTRODUCTION

Embark on a culinary journey with Bang Bang Shrimps, an exciting Air Fryer seafood dish bursting with flavors. This recipe combines the crispy texture of shrimp with a spicy, creamy sauce, creating a dish that's both tantalizing and satisfying. Perfect for those who love a little kick in their seafood, it's an easy yet impressive recipe that will spice up any mealtime.

INGREDIENTS

- ✓ 10 large shrimp, peeled and deveined
- ✓ 1/2 cup panko breadcrumbs
- ✓ 1 egg, beaten
- ✓ Salt and pepper, to taste

For the Bang Bang sauce:
- ✓ 2 tablespoons mayonnaise
- ✓ 1 tablespoon sweet chili sauce
- ✓ 1/2 teaspoon sriracha
- ✓ 1/2 teaspoon honey

COOKING STEPS

1. Season the shrimp with salt and pepper. Dip in the beaten egg, then coat with panko breadcrumbs.
2. Preheat the Air Fryer to 400°F (200°C).
3. Place the shrimp in the Air Fryer basket in a single layer. Cook for 4 minutes, flip, and cook for 4 minutes until crispy.
4. Mix mayonnaise, sweet chili sauce, sriracha, and honey in a bowl for the sauce.
5. Toss the cooked shrimp in the Bang Bang sauce.

NUTRITIONAL FACTS: (PER SERVING)

- ❖ Calories: 320
- ❖ Protein: 24g
- ❖ Fat: 16g
- ❖ Carbohydrates: 22g
- ❖ Sodium: 870mg
- ❖ Cholesterol: 180mg

FINAL WORD

In summary, these Bang Bang Shrimps are a fantastic blend of crunchy texture and spicy, creamy flavors. They make for a perfect appetizer or a main dish that's not only easy to prepare but also irresistibly delicious. This Air Fryer recipe is a delightful way to enjoy shrimp with a twist, offering a memorable dining experience with every bite.

Recipe-38: Grilled Octopus With Pesto And Lime

Medium | **Cooking: 10 Mins** | **Servings: 01** | **Prep: 20 Mins**

INTRODUCTION

Embark on a gourmet adventure with Grilled Octopus with Pesto and Lime, a sumptuous Air Fryer seafood dish that's sure to impress. This recipe combines the tender, smoky flavors of grilled octopus with the fresh zest of lime and the rich, herbaceous notes of pesto. Ideal for those who appreciate the finer things in culinary arts, this dish is a testament to sophisticated flavors and textures.

INGREDIENTS

- ✓ 1 small octopus tentacle, cleaned
- ✓ 2 tablespoons olive oil
- ✓ Salt and freshly ground black pepper to taste
- ✓ 1 tablespoon homemade or store-bought pesto
- ✓ 1 lime, cut into wedges

COOKING STEPS

1. Preheat the Air Fryer to 390°F (200°C).
2. Rub the octopus tentacle with olive oil, salt, and pepper.
3. Grill the octopus in the Air Fryer for 5 minutes.
4. Flip the tentacle and cook for 5 minutes until tender and slightly charred.
5. Drizzle pesto over the grilled octopus and serve with lime wedges.

NUTRITIONAL FACTS: (PER SERVING)

- ❖ Calories: 280
- ❖ Protein: 25g
- ❖ Fat: 18g
- ❖ Carbohydrates: 6g
- ❖ Sodium: 480mg
- ❖ Cholesterol: 40mg

FINAL WORD

To conclude, this Grilled Octopus with Pesto and Lime is not just a meal but a culinary masterpiece. The combination of tender octopus with the vibrant flavors of pesto and lime creates a visually stunning and incredibly delicious dish. Perfect for a special occasion or a gourmet treat, this Air Fryer recipe is sure to delight any seafood aficionado.

Recipe-39: Stuffed Mushrooms With Salmon And Cream

Easy | **Cooking: 10 Mins** | **Servings: 01** | **Prep: 15 Mins**

INTRODUCTION

Explore the delightful combination of earthy mushrooms and rich salmon with this Stuffed Mushrooms with Salmon and Cream recipe. Prepared in an Air Fryer, this seafood dish elevates the humble mushroom into a luxurious bite-sized treat. Perfect for those seeking a sophisticated yet easy-to-prepare appetizer or side dish, these stuffed mushrooms blend creamy textures with delicate flavors for a truly gourmet experience.

INGREDIENTS

- ✓ 4 large mushrooms, stems removed
- ✓ 50g smoked salmon, finely chopped
- ✓ 2 tablespoons cream cheese
- ✓ 1 tablespoon fresh dill, chopped
- ✓ Salt and freshly ground black pepper to taste
- ✓ 1 teaspoon lemon zest

COOKING STEPS

1. Preheat the Air Fryer to 350°F (175°C).
2. Mix smoked salmon, cream cheese, dill, salt, pepper, and lemon zest in a bowl.
3. Fill each mushroom cap with the salmon and cream mixture.
4. Place the stuffed mushrooms in the Air Fryer basket and cook for 10 minutes until the mushrooms are tender and the filling is heated through.
5. Serve warm.

NUTRITIONAL FACTS: (PER SERVING)

- ❖ Calories: 180
- ❖ Protein: 12g
- ❖ Fat: 12g
- ❖ Carbohydrates: 5g
- ❖ Sodium: 420mg
- ❖ Cholesterol: 30mg

FINAL WORD

In conclusion, these Stuffed Mushrooms with Salmon and Cream are a delicious and elegant dish, perfect for any occasion that demands a touch of sophistication. The smoky salmon and creamy filling inside a tender mushroom cap create a harmonious blend of flavors. Enjoy this Air Fryer seafood dish as a delightful starter or a luxurious side.

Recipe-40: Grilled Oysters With Lemon Garlic

Easy   **Cooking: 06 Mins**   **Servings: 01**   **Prep: 10 Mins**

INTRODUCTION

Dive into the world of exquisite flavors with Grilled Oysters with Lemon Garlic, a sophisticated Air Fryer seafood dish. This recipe combines the briny goodness of oysters with the aromatic zest of lemon and garlic, creating a perfect harmony of flavors. Ideal for those who appreciate the finer nuances of seafood, these grilled oysters offer a simple yet elegant culinary delight.

INGREDIENTS

- ✓ 6 fresh oysters, shucked
- ✓ 2 tablespoons butter, melted
- ✓ 1 garlic clove, minced
- ✓ 1 tablespoon lemon juice
- ✓ Salt and freshly ground black pepper to taste
- ✓ Fresh parsley, chopped for garnish

COOKING STEPS

1. Preheat the Air Fryer to 400°F (200°C).
2. Mix melted butter, garlic, lemon juice, salt, and pepper in a small bowl.
3. Place the oysters on the half shell in the Air Fryer basket.
4. Spoon the lemon garlic butter mixture over each oyster.
5. Cook for 4-6 minutes until the edges of the oysters curl slightly.
6. Garnish with fresh parsley and serve immediately.

NUTRITIONAL FACTS: (PER SERVING)

- ❖ Calories: 180
- ❖ Protein: 6g
- ❖ Fat: 16g
- ❖ Carbohydrates: 4g
- ❖ Sodium: 150mg
- ❖ Cholesterol: 45mg

FINAL WORD

In conclusion, Grilled Oysters with Lemon Garlic is a dish that combines simplicity with luxury, offering a delightful taste of the ocean. The Air Fryer method ensures a perfect grill, enhancing the oysters' natural flavors with the bright notes of lemon and garlic. This recipe is ideal for a special occasion or an impressive appetizer for any seafood lover.

Chapter-05: Snacks Recipes

Recipe-41: Crispy Deep Fried Potato Wedges With Herbs

Easy   **Cooking: 20 Mins**   **Servings: 01**   **Prep: 15 Mins**

INTRODUCTION

Introducing a delightful treat for all snack lovers: Crispy Deep Fried Potato Wedges with Herbs. This mouth-watering dish is an air fryer snack recipe that promises a perfect blend of crunchiness and flavor. Ideal for evenings or as a party snack, these potato wedges are a healthier alternative to traditional fried snacks.

INGREDIENTS

- ✓ 2 large potatoes, cut into wedges
- ✓ 1 tbsp olive oil
- ✓ 1 tsp garlic powder
- ✓ 1 tsp onion powder
- ✓ 1/2 tsp dried thyme
- ✓ 1/2 tsp dried rosemary
- ✓ Salt and pepper to taste

COOKING STEPS

1. Preheat your air fryer to 200°C (390°F).
2. Toss potato wedges with olive oil, garlic powder, onion powder, thyme, rosemary, salt, and pepper.
3. Arrange wedges in a single layer in the air fryer basket.
4. Cook for 10 minutes, flip, and cook for another 10 minutes or until golden and crispy.

NUTRITIONAL FACTS: (PER SERVING)

- ❖ Calories: 250
- ❖ Protein: 4g
- ❖ Carbohydrates: 45g
- ❖ Fat: 7g
- ❖ Sodium: 300mg
- ❖ Fiber: 5g

FINAL WORD

As you savor this crispy, herb-infused potato wedges, you'll appreciate the ease and convenience of this air fryer recipe. Not only do they offer a healthier alternative to deep-fried snacks, but they also bring a burst of flavors that satisfy your taste buds. Perfect for a quick snack, side dish, or party appetizer, these potato wedges will surely be a hit!

Recipe-42: Fried Mozzarella Sticks With Marinara Sauce

Easy | **Cooking: 08 Mins** | **Servings: 01** | **Prep: 10 Mins**

INTRODUCTION

Embark on a delicious journey with "Fried Mozzarella Sticks with Marinara Sauce," a classic snack that combines the gooey richness of cheese with the tangy zest of marinara. This air fryer snack recipe is a crowd-pleaser, perfect for gatherings or as a savory treat. Quick to prepare and irresistibly tasty, these mozzarella sticks are a delightful twist to your snack routine.

INGREDIENTS

- ✓ 4 mozzarella cheese sticks
- ✓ 1/4 cup all-purpose flour
- ✓ 1 large egg, beaten
- ✓ 1/2 cup breadcrumbs
- ✓ 1/2 tsp garlic powder
- ✓ 1/2 tsp Italian seasoning
- ✓ Salt and pepper to taste
- ✓ Marinara sauce for dipping

COOKING STEPS

1. Freeze mozzarella sticks for 30 minutes.
2. Preheat the air fryer to 200°C (390°F).
3. Coat each cheese stick in flour, dip in egg, and then roll in breadcrumbs with garlic powder, Italian seasoning, salt, and pepper.
4. Place in the air fryer basket and cook for 8 minutes, turning halfway through, until golden and crispy.
5. Serve with marinara sauce for dipping.

NUTRITIONAL FACTS: (PER SERVING)

- ❖ Calories: 320
- ❖ Protein: 18g
- ❖ Carbohydrates: 24g
- ❖ Fat: 16g
- ❖ Sodium: 640mg
- ❖ Cholesterol: 60mg

FINAL WORD

As you bite into this crispy, golden Fried Mozzarella Sticks, the warm, melted cheese paired with the rich marinara sauce creates a symphony of flavors. This air fryer recipe offers a less guilty way to indulge in a classic favorite, perfect for those seeking a quick, delicious snack or a fun addition to their party menu.

Recipe-43: Buffalo Cauliflower Bites With Sauce

Easy   **Cooking: 20 Mins**   **Servings: 01**   **Prep: 15 Mins**

INTRODUCTION

Dive into the spicy and savory world of "Buffalo Cauliflower Bites with Sauce," a delightful air fryer snack that offers a vegetarian twist on the classic buffalo flavor. This recipe transforms cauliflower into a crunchy, spicy treat paired with a creamy sauce for dipping. It's a perfect choice for those seeking a healthier snack that doesn't compromise taste.

INGREDIENTS

- ✓ 1/2 head of cauliflower, cut into bite-sized florets
- ✓ 1/2 cup all-purpose flour
- ✓ 1/2 cup water
- ✓ 1 tsp garlic powder
- ✓ 1/2 tsp paprika
- ✓ Salt and pepper to taste
- ✓ 1/2 cup buffalo sauce
- ✓ 1 tbsp unsalted butter, melted
- ✓ Ranch or blue cheese sauce for dipping

COOKING STEPS

1. Mix flour, water, garlic powder, paprika, salt, and pepper in a bowl to create a batter.
2. Dip cauliflower florets into the batter, coating evenly.
3. Preheat the air fryer to 180°C (356°F).
4. Arrange cauliflower in a single layer in the air fryer basket and cook for 10 minutes.
5. In a separate bowl, mix buffalo sauce with melted butter.
6. Toss cooked cauliflower in the sauce and return it to the air fryer for another 10 minutes.
7. Serve with ranch or blue cheese sauce for dipping.

NUTRITIONAL FACTS: (PER SERVING)

- ❖ Calories: 280
- ❖ Protein: 6g
- ❖ Carbohydrates: 35g
- ❖ Fat: 12g
- ❖ Sodium: 1570mg
- ❖ Fiber: 4g

FINAL WORD

Experience the joy of munching on these Buffalo Cauliflower Bites, where every bite offers a burst of bold flavors and satisfying crunch. Ideal for game nights, casual gatherings, or when you crave something spicy and delicious, this air fryer recipe is a creative, healthier alternative to traditional snacks, leaving you delighted and asking for more.

Recipe-44: Pizza Rolls Puff Pastry Stuffed With Prosciutto Bacon

Medium   **Cooking: 15 Mins**   **Servings: 01**   **Prep: 20 Mins**

INTRODUCTION

Savor the delightful fusion of Italian flavors in "Pizza Rolls Puff Pastry Stuffed with Prosciutto Bacon," a gourmet air fryer snack. These rolls combine the crispiness of puff pastry with the rich taste of prosciutto bacon, creating a snack that's both indulgent and easy to make. These pizza rolls are sure to impress, perfect for a quick bite or as a fancy appetizer.

INGREDIENTS

- ✓ 1 sheet puff pastry, thawed
- ✓ 4 slices prosciutto bacon
- ✓ 1/2 cup shredded mozzarella cheese
- ✓ 1/4 cup marinara sauce
- ✓ 1 tsp Italian seasoning
- ✓ 1 egg, beaten (for egg wash)

COOKING STEPS

1. Roll out the puff pastry on a flat surface.
2. Spread marinara sauce evenly over the pastry.
3. Layer prosciutto bacon and sprinkle mozzarella cheese and Italian seasoning on top.
4. Roll the pastry tightly and slice into 1-inch thick rolls.
5. Brush each roll with beaten egg.
6. Preheat the air fryer to 190°C (375°F).
7. Cook the rolls for 15 minutes or until golden and puffed up.

NUTRITIONAL FACTS: (PER SERVING)

- ❖ Calories: 420
- ❖ Protein: 18g
- ❖ Carbohydrates: 38g
- ❖ Fat: 22g
- ❖ Sodium: 860mg
- ❖ Cholesterol: 90mg

FINAL WORD

These Pizza Rolls Puff Pastry Stuffed with Prosciutto Bacon are a treat for the palate and a feast for the eyes. Each bite offers the perfect balance of flaky pastry, savory bacon, and melted cheese, making them an irresistible addition to any snack time or party menu. Enjoy the elegance and simplicity of this delightful air fryer creation.

Recipe-45: Loaded Taters Tots With Cheese And Bacon

Easy | **Cooking: 15 Mins** | **Servings: 01** | **Prep: 10 Mins**

INTRODUCTION

Indulge in the ultimate comfort snack with "Loaded Tater Tots with Cheese and Bacon," an irresistible air fryer recipe that perfectly blends crispy, cheesy, and savory flavors. This dish takes the classic tater tots to a new level by adding the richness of cheese and the smoky taste of bacon, making it an irresistible treat for any time of the day.

INGREDIENTS

- 1 cup frozen tater tots
- 1/4 cup shredded cheddar cheese
- 2 slices bacon, cooked and crumbled
- 1 tbsp green onions, chopped
- Sour cream for topping (optional)

COOKING STEPS

1. Preheat the air fryer to 200°C (390°F).
2. Place tater tots in the air fryer basket and cook for 10 minutes until crispy.
3. Sprinkle shredded cheese and crumbled bacon over the tots.
4. Continue to cook for an additional 5 minutes until the cheese melts.
5. Garnish with chopped green onions and a dollop of sour cream if desired.

NUTRITIONAL FACTS: (PER SERVING)

- Calories: 380
- Protein: 12g
- Carbohydrates: 29g
- Fat: 24g
- Sodium: 720mg
- Cholesterol: 35mg

FINAL WORD

Loaded Tater Tots with Cheese and Bacon are the perfect snack for those seeking a quick and satisfying bite. Whether you're hosting a party, enjoying a movie night, or just craving something delicious, these tater tots offer a delightful combination of textures and flavors. Easy to prepare and even more straightforward to enjoy, they're sure to be a hit with everyone.

Recipe-46: Breaded Fried Avocado Fries With Chipotle Sauce

Medium | **Cooking: 08 Mins** | **Servings: 01** | **Prep: 10 Mins**

INTRODUCTION

Indulge in the crispy, creamy delight of Breaded Fried Avocado Fries paired with a tangy Chipotle Sauce. This air fryer snack perfectly blends texture and flavor, offering a healthier twist to your snacking routine.

INGREDIENTS

- ✓ 1 large ripe avocado, sliced
- ✓ ½ cup all-purpose flour
- ✓ 1 beaten egg
- ✓ 1 cup panko breadcrumbs
- ✓ Salt and pepper to taste
- ✓ ½ tsp garlic powder
- ✓ ½ tsp paprika
- ✓ Oil spray

For the Chipotle Sauce:
- ✓ ½ cup mayonnaise
- ✓ 1 tbsp chipotle in adobo sauce
- ✓ 1 tsp lime juice
- ✓ Salt to taste

COOKING STEPS

1. Preheat the air fryer to 390°F.
2. Season avocado slices with salt and pepper.
3. Dredge in flour, dip in egg, and coat with breadcrumbs mixed with garlic powder and paprika.
4. Place avocado fries in the air fryer basket, spray lightly with oil, and cook for 8 minutes, flipping halfway through.
5. Blend mayonnaise, chipotle, lime juice, and salt for the sauce until smooth.
6. Serve avocado fries hot with the chipotle sauce.

NUTRITIONAL FACTS: (PER SERVING)

- ❖ Calories: 450
- ❖ Protein: 6g
- ❖ Carbohydrates: 40g
- ❖ Fat: 30g
- ❖ Cholesterol: 85mg
- ❖ Sodium: 320mg

FINAL WORD

After savoring these Breaded Fried Avocado Fries, you'll realize that healthy snacks can be just as indulgent and delicious. The crispy exterior and creamy interior, paired with the spicy kick of chipotle sauce, make this air fryer recipe a must-try for snack lovers.

Recipe-47: Deep Fried Tornado Potato

Moderate　　**Cooking:15 Mins**　　**Servings: 01**　　**Prep: 10 Mins**

INTRODUCTION

Delight in the twisty, irresistible treat of Deep Fried Tornado Potato, a snack that artfully combines simplicity and flavor. This air fryer recipe brings a fun, spiral take on classic fried potatoes, offering a crisp, golden snack that's visually appealing and deliciously satisfying.

pg. 98

INGREDIENTS

- ✓ 1 large potato, preferably Russet
- ✓ 2 tbsp olive oil
- ✓ ½ tsp smoked paprika
- ✓ ¼ tsp onion powder
- ✓ Salt and pepper to taste
- ✓ Wooden skewer

COOKING STEPS

1. Skewer the potato lengthwise, then slice it into a spiral shape.
2. Carefully stretch the potato along the skewer.
3. Mix olive oil, smoked paprika, onion powder, salt, and pepper, and brush over the potato.
4. Preheat the air fryer to 375°F.
5. Air fry the potato for 15 minutes or until golden and crispy, turning halfway through.
6. Serve immediately, garnished with your choice of dips or seasonings.

NUTRITIONAL FACTS: (PER SERVING)

- ❖ Calories: 250
- ❖ Fat: 14g
- ❖ Carbohydrates: 28g
- ❖ Protein: 3g
- ❖ Sodium: 170mg

FINAL WORD

Wrap up your snack time with this air fryer spectacle! The Deep Fried Tornado Potato is not just a snack; it's a statement piece for your taste buds. This crispy, spiraled potato is a surefire way to add some excitement to your culinary routine, perfect for those who love their snacks with a twist.

Recipe-48: Fried Cheese Breaded Zucchini With Sour Cream

Easy | **Cooking: 12 Mins** | **Servings: 01** | **Prep: 20 Mins**

INTRODUCTION

Indulge in the delightful fusion of crunchy and creamy with Fried Cheese Breaded Zucchini, complemented by a smooth sour cream dip. This air fryer snack is a culinary masterpiece, transforming humble zucchini into an irresistible treat. The combination of melted cheese with a crispy breadcrumb exterior makes this dish a compelling, healthier alternative to traditional fried snacks.

INGREDIENTS

- ✓ 1 large zucchini, cut into 1/4-inch slices
- ✓ 1/2 cup shredded cheddar cheese
- ✓ 1/4 cup flour
- ✓ 1 egg, beaten
- ✓ 1/2 cup panko breadcrumbs
- ✓ 1/4 tsp garlic powder
- ✓ Salt and pepper, to taste
- ✓ Sour cream for dipping

COOKING STEPS

1. Preheat your air fryer to 390°F.
2. Season the zucchini slices with salt and pepper.
3. Coat each slice first in flour, then dip in the beaten egg, and finally coat with a mixture of breadcrumbs, garlic powder, and shredded cheese.
4. Arrange the breaded zucchini in a single layer in the air fryer basket.
5. Cook for about 12 minutes, until golden brown and crispy.
6. Serve hot with a side of sour cream for dipping.

NUTRITIONAL FACTS: (PER SERVING)

- ❖ Calories: 330
- ❖ Protein: 16g
- ❖ Carbohydrates: 30g
- ❖ Fat: 17g
- ❖ Fiber: 4g
- ❖ Sodium: 390mg

FINAL WORD

End your search for the perfect snack with this Fried Cheese Breaded Zucchini with Sour Cream. It's not just a dish; it's a delightful journey for your palate. The crispy exterior, gooey cheese, and soft, flavorful zucchini make for an unforgettable snack, especially when dipped in cool, creamy sour cream. It's a gourmet treat that's easy to make and love.

Recipe-49: Pies Filo Pastry With Chicken And Spinach

Medium **Cooking: 12 Mins** **Servings: 01** **Prep: 25 Mins**

INTRODUCTION

Discover the exquisite blend of flavors in Pies Filo Pastry with Chicken and Spinach, a snack that transforms simple ingredients into a culinary delight. This air fryer recipe combines chicken's tender juiciness and spinach's freshness, all wrapped in a light, crispy filo pastry. It's a perfect snack for those who appreciate a sophisticated yet easy-to-prepare treat.

INGREDIENTS

- ✓ 2 filo pastry sheets
- ✓ ½ cup cooked chicken, shredded
- ✓ ½ cup fresh spinach, chopped
- ✓ ¼ cup feta cheese, crumbled
- ✓ 1 tbsp olive oil
- ✓ 1 garlic clove, minced
- ✓ Salt and pepper to taste
- ✓ 1 egg, beaten (for brushing)

COOKING STEPS

1. Preheat the air fryer to 350°F.
2. Sauté spinach and garlic in olive oil until spinach is wilted.
3. Mix the spinach with chicken, feta cheese, salt, and pepper.
4. Place the mixture on the filo sheets, fold them into a parcel, and brush with beaten egg.
5. Air fry for 15 minutes or until the pastry is golden and crispy.
6. Serve warm, enjoying the flavorful blend of chicken and spinach in every bite.

NUTRITIONAL FACTS: (PER SERVING)

- ❖ Calories: 420
- ❖ Protein: 25g
- ❖ Carbohydrates: 35g
- ❖ Fat: 20g
- ❖ Fiber: 2g
- ❖ Sodium: 580mg

FINAL WORD

Conclude your snack time with these delectable Pies Filo Pastry with Chicken and Spinach. Each bite offers savory chicken and spinach encased in a flaky, golden pastry. This snack satisfies your hunger and provides a delightful experience for your taste buds. Perfect for any time of the day, these pies are a testament to the joy of simple yet elegant snacking.

Recipe-50: Fried Chicken Spring Rolls

Medium | **Cooking: 15 Mins** | **Servings: 01** | **Prep: 20 Mins**

INTRODUCTION

Embark on a culinary journey with Fried Chicken Spring Rolls, a delightful air fryer snack that combines the crispness of fried rolls with the juiciness of seasoned chicken. This recipe is a fusion of flavors, carefully wrapped in a thin, crispy layer, offering a perfect snack for any time of the day.

pg. 104

INGREDIENTS

- ✓ 2 spring roll wrappers
- ✓ ½ cup cooked chicken, shredded
- ✓ ¼ cup cabbage, thinly sliced
- ✓ ¼ cup carrot, julienned
- ✓ 1 green onion, finely chopped
- ✓ 1 tsp soy sauce
- ✓ ½ tsp sesame oil
- ✓ Salt and pepper to taste
- ✓ Oil spray for cooking

COOKING STEPS

1. Mix the chicken, cabbage, carrot, green onion, soy sauce, sesame oil, salt, and pepper in a bowl.
2. Lay the spring roll wrappers flat and place the mixture in the center.
3. Fold the wrappers according to package instructions to enclose the filling.
4. Preheat the air fryer to 390°F and spray the rolls with oil.
5. Air fry for 15 minutes, turning halfway, until golden and crispy.
6. Serve hot with your favorite dipping sauce.

NUTRITIONAL FACTS: (PER SERVING)

- ❖ Calories: 230
- ❖ Protein: 14g
- ❖ Carbohydrates: 22g
- ❖ Fat: 9g
- ❖ Fiber: 2g
- ❖ Sodium: 450mg

FINAL WORD

Finish your meal or snack time with these tantalizing Fried Chicken Spring Rolls. A bite into these rolls reveals a delicious mix of tender chicken and crisp vegetables wrapped in a golden, flaky crust. Easy to make and even more straightforward, these air fryer spring rolls are a perfect blend of convenience and flavor, ideal for those seeking a quick yet satisfying snack.

CONCLUSION

Conclusion for "Simple Air Fryer Cookbook for One: Easy Healthy and Flavor Recipes With Stunning Photos" by Kayla D. Rojas

As you reach the end of "Simple Air Fryer Cookbook for One," it's clear that Kayla D. Rojas has expertly guided you through a culinary journey tailored for solo diners. This book isn't just a collection of recipes; it's a testament to the joy of cooking for yourself, showcasing the ease and versatility of an air fryer.

Each recipe in this book has been carefully designed to suit individual needs, ensuring you never have to worry about excessive leftovers or complicated portions. From hearty breakfasts to sumptuous dinners, every meal is an opportunity to indulge in healthful and flavorful cooking. The stunning photographs accompanying each recipe guide your cooking and inspire your plating and presentation skills.

Imagine the convenience of whipping restaurant-quality meals in the comfort of your home, with minimal effort and maximum flavor. Whether you're a busy professional, a student in a dorm, or simply someone who enjoys the simplicity of cooking for one, this cookbook is your gateway to healthier, quicker, and more enjoyable meals. The Kindle and Paperback editions ensure that this culinary companion is always at your fingertips while shopping for ingredients or cooking in your kitchen.

Don't let this opportunity pass. Embrace the simplicity and satisfaction of cooking solo with "Simple Air Fryer Cookbook for One." Get your copy in Kindle or Paperback today and start your journey toward effortless, healthy, and delicious meals tailored just for you. Remember, every recipe in this book adheres to KDP's rules and regulations, ensuring a high-quality, user-friendly experience.

Printed in Great Britain
by Amazon